Chichester
A Walk in the City

Sue Finniss

with architectural descriptions by

John Elliott

and a foreword by

Anne Scicluna
Mayor of Chichester

Spire Books Ltd
PO Box 2336, Reading RG4 5WJ
www.spirebooks.com

CIP data: a catalogue record for this book is avail-
able from the British Library

Designed by John Elliott
ISBN 978-1-904965-39-8

Contents

Forewords 7

Chichester: A Brief History 10

The Cathedral

Cathedral Church of the Holy Trinity 16

The Cathedral Interior 18

St Richard of Chichester 20

Bell Tower 22

The Cloisters & the Chapel of St Faith 24

Cathedral from St Richard's Walk 26

Cathedral Spire from Refectory Garden 28

George Bell House 30

Palace Gate 32

Bishop's Palace 34

Vicars' Close 36

Canon Gate 38

The City

Market Cross 42

All Saints in the Pallant 44

West Pallant 46

Pallant House 48

St John the Evangelist 50

Corn Exchange 52

St Andrew, Oxmarket 54

The Dolphin & Anchor 56

St Peter the Great 58

Ede's House 60

Market House 62

St Olave's Church 64

Council House & Assembly Rooms 66

Greyfriars or Guildhall 68

St Mary's Hospital 70

St Martin's Square 72

Chichester Festival Theatre 74

Out & About

Chichester's Canal 78

Holy Trinity, Bosham 80

Sailing in Chichester Harbour 82

Roman Palace, Fishbourne 84

West Dean 86

West Dean Gardens 88

Chichester Harbour 90

Cottages in Franklin Place

Forewords

Having been born and brought up in Chichester, and now serving my third term as Mayor, I own a large number of books on the city. I, and a number of my colleagues who have also served as Mayor, have found that there are few publications which are of a non-specialist nature showing the city as it is today. We do, of course, greatly value books telling of our city's rich history and heritage, showing old photographs and detailed text. However, these are often not what visitors want – they may well wish to have something as a valued memento of their stay, showing pictures of what they have actually seen whilst staying with us.

Here is a book which fits the bill perfectly. It is a book which can be bought by or given to visitors to our city, whether they are local or from overseas. With beautifully executed watercolour paintings of local places of interest and short descriptions, it will bring back to visitors memories of a happy stay in our city, and for Chichester residents it will be a very welcome addition to their collection of local books.

Anne Scicluna
Mayor of Chichester
July 2012

With the cooperation of John Elliott and Spire Books I have already completed two books illustrating my home city of Salisbury, so I was pleased to extend my work to Chichester.

I have a special affection for the city for two reasons. It was here that I began to paint seriously in watercolours. In about 1979 I attended a summer school at what was then known as Bishop Otter College. I remember that the tutor chose the terrace of coloured cottages in Franklin Place as our first subject. I have never looked back! There is also my enthusiasm for nearby West Dean College where, during one of their courses, I had a life-changing conversation with a fellow student who encouraged me to give up my job as a head teacher and to devote all my time to painting.

It has been a great pleasure to become more familiar with Chichester whilst choosing appropriate places to illustrate. Some have been selected for their historical or architectural interest, others simply for their artistic appeal. I have particularly enjoyed discovering the Chichester Canal and the point from where Turner made his painting. I am very grateful to the kind lady who saw me photographing St Mary's hospital and, as a key holder, took me into the garden and showed me the chapel.

Sue Finniss
July 2012

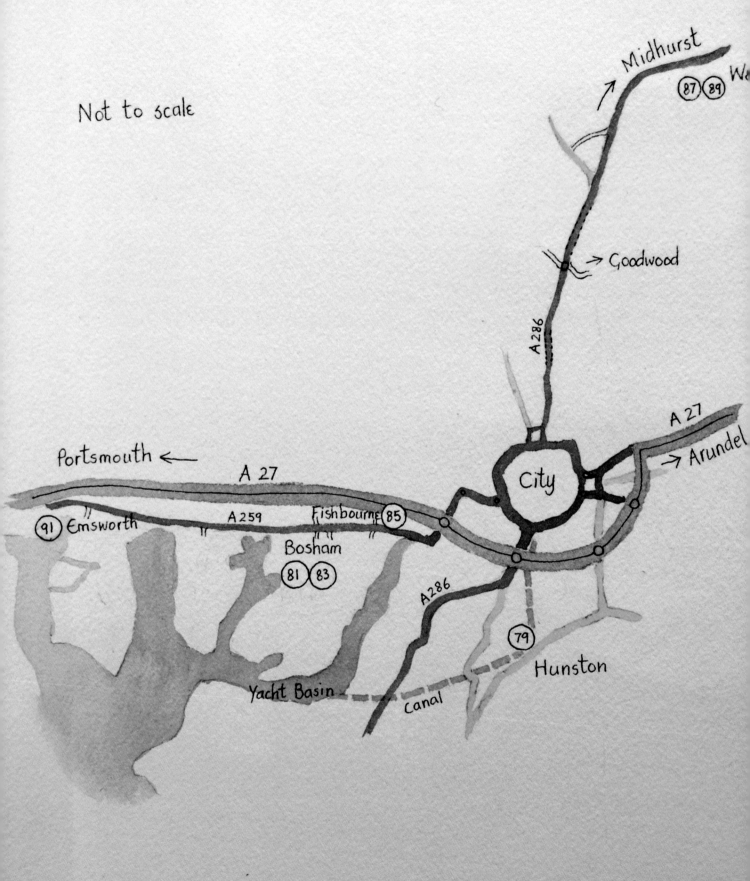

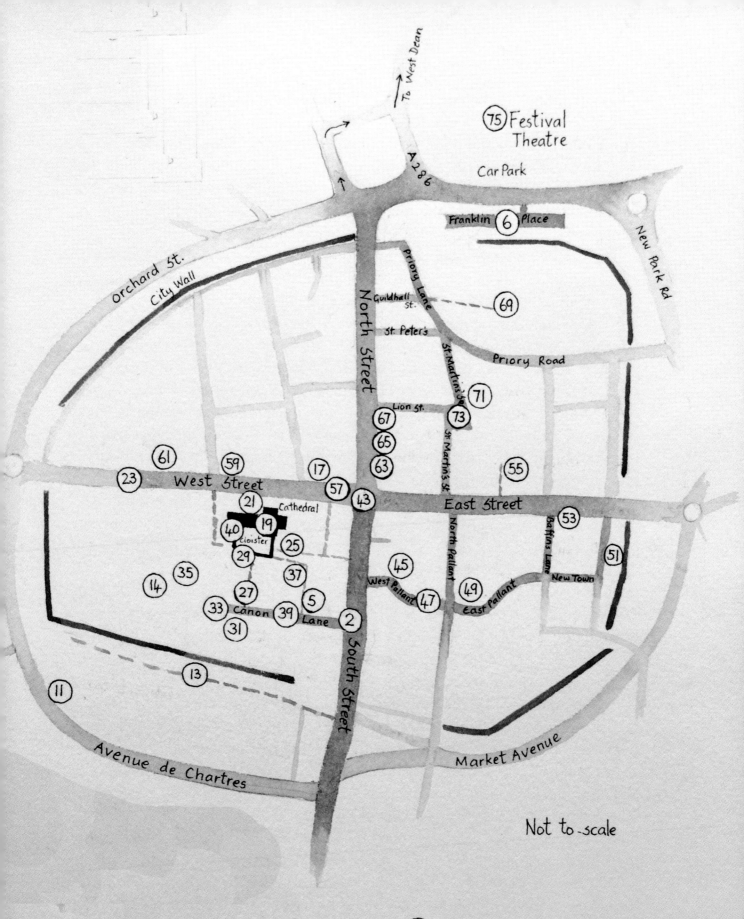

Not to-scale

(8) indicates the page number of the illustration and the approximate position from where the painting was made.

Chichester: A Brief History

Modern Chichester has a population of about 23,000 and occupies a strategic position on the south coast. Local government is centred here, it is a communications hub, a significant sailing area and a major cultural centre as well as being a bishopric within the Church of England and the location of an important twelfth century Cathedral.

The origins of Chichester most probably date from around the first century BC when there was a migration from the chalkland hills to the more fertile plain below. Certainly a settlement of some size existed when the Romans arrived in AD43. The locals did not appear to greatly oppose the new arrivals and Chichester became important as a Roman settlement.

There was a Roman palace at Fishbourne, which is just to the west of the city and at the head of Chichester Harbour, and the current city centre stands on the foundations of the Roman city of Noviomagus Regensium that acted as the capital for the surrounding area. Remnants of an amphitheatre, that was built just outside the east gate of the old Roman city walls, are still partly visible. The Roman period was most probably also responsible for the gridiron street pattern that radiates from the Market Cross and a Roman Forum possibly existed on a site near the junction of North and West Streets. The fact that the city walls were only built at the end of the second century suggests that the Roman settlement was not threatened by others. The city walls that are visible today are a medieval rebuilding on the Roman foundations. Four city gates were removed in 1772-83.

The Anglo-Saxons followed towards the end of the fifth century when the city became the chief occupied area in the Kingdom of Sussex and was called Cissan Ceaster. It was one of the fortified towns created by Alfred the Great in 878-9 and was home to the South Saxon kings for over 300 years.

A consequence of the Battle of Hastings and Norman occupation was that the city was given to Roger de Mongomerie as a reward for his assistance. The Domesday Book shows Chichester with 300 dwellings suggesting a population of about 1,500. Chichester Castle was built and the city was fortified in 1104.

The Cathedral for the South Saxons was created at Selsey in 681 and it was not until 1075 that the bishopric was moved, to the eaily defensibly Chichester. Much the same happened in Salisbury when the Cathedral was moved from Sherborne to Old Sarum around 1075 before being relocated to its current position in the valley below in 1220. Like most Cathedral cities, Chichester is dominated by its Cathedral, though around this lies a modern city which has developed out of the past, and especially out of the eighteenth and nineteenth century redevelopments.

The Market Cross originates from 1501, the Council House from 1731, the Butter Market in North Street from 1808, and the Corn Exchange 1833.

The notes produced by James Sparshott, a member of the Baptist community, tells us that in the early 1700s the city was dominated by old, low, timber-built, houses with shops that were open to the street. Little London was 'very dirty', Pallant 'very old and full of malt-houses'. Bull-baiting, wrestling, cudgelling, cock-fighting, dog-fights and badger-baiting seem to have been the most prominent popular pastimes. Then about 1724 a process of rebuilding started; both civic and private. The Market House was taken down and a new one built in 1731, and by 1784 Sparshott tells us that the 'whole city was built or new faced' with the fashionable brick.

As is often the case in Cathedral cities, religion of all varieties played a significant role. At one time in the twentieth century the city had fifteen churches, most of which were Anglican. In more recent times many churches have had to find new uses. The Anglican St John the Evangelist (1812-13) rests peacefully as a redundant church while its cousin St Peter the Great in West Street (1848-52) is now a pub!

Modern Chichester is also important for its cultural life. Leonard Bernstein wrote his *Chichester Psalms* for the 1965 Southern Cathedrals Festival which was held in the Cathedral. Slightly to the north of the city lies the prestigious Chichester Festival Theatre that has attracted some of the greatest actors and producers. If that were not enough there is the annual Chichester Festivities, a three-week arts and music festival, a symphony orchestra and a Real Ale and Jazz Festival which attracts top jazz musicians.

Chichester has always been important for its market and as a centre for the local corn trade. Its position close to the head of the navigable Chichester Harbour added another dimension to its influence, though in his *A Tour Through the Whole Island of Great Britain*, published between 1724-6, Daniel Defoe quipped that the 'city is not a place of much trade, nor is it very populous' and 'if six or seven good families were removed, there would not be much conversation, except what is to be found among the canons, and dignitaries of the Cathedral'. He recounted that the surrounding countryside was 'very fruitful, and particularly in good wheat'. The local farmers used to take their produce to market at Farnham but some local businessmen had built large granaries at Crook that fed the local mills and generated a sea trade with London. The abundant surviving Georgian heritage tends to contradict Defoe and suggests that this was a prosperous place in the late-eighteenth century and home to many affluent merchants.

A leafy walk near the City walls

The Cathedral

Cathedral Church of the Holy Trinity

Chichester Cathedral is significant on at least three counts. Unlike many English Cathedrals it can be seen from miles around, standing proudly as a proclamation of its existence. Secondly, it is the product of evolution and change over many centuries; a product of the constant need to adapt. Thirdly, there is little visual or structural separation between the Cathedral and its adjoining city: no great wall, no ditch, nothing to formally mark out a separation of religious and secular authority.

It was in 1075 that the see was moved from Selsey to Chichester and work soon started on the creation of a new Cathedral, most likely on the site of an earlier Saxon parish church. This was probably incorporated into the north transept where it remained until 1848-52 when the parish worship was moved to the new, and adjacent, St Peter the Great. Most of the original Cathedral building work was undertaken during the period that Bishop Ralph de Luffa (bishop 1091-1123) was in charge and the building was dedicated in 1108. The city and Cathedral were severely damaged by a great fire in 1114 and the roof was destroyed. Restoration and rebuilding followed and was completed by 1125. There was another fire in 1187 and the Cathedral was repaired, then consecrated again in 1199 and dedicated to the Holy Trinity.

The initial structure comprised an eight-bay nave with two western towers, transepts and a three-bay presbytery with an apsidal ambulatory at the eastern end. Building work, with changes and additions, continued into the thirteenth century. Side chapels were added on the south (c.1225) and north (c.1275) and the central tower heightened (c.1250). A storm wrecked two towers in 1210 so that needed to be rebuilt, the Lady Chapel was added around 1288-1305 when the eastern-most bays of the Norman Cathedral were rebuilt in the Gothic style. The spire was built around 1400 and the cloisters along with the detached bell tower were added about 1436. The spire and tower collapsed in a gale during 1861, probably a consequence of restoration work, but were rebuilt in the original style. The other nineteenth century restoration work included the introduction of a great west window and another in the north transept. The north-west tower was replaced in 1901. The result of all this work changed the original structure, chiefly by adding the five bay Lady Chapel at the eastern end and removing the apsidal termination that had existed.

The original building stone was a mix of local material and that from Quarr Abbey on the Isle of Wight, with Caen stone being used for the subsequent modifications and additions.

Stylistically the Cathedral is an eclectic mix, though some claim that the dominant spirit is Norman as was the original Cathedral. However, the detail is often Gothic; a little Early English here, a little Decorated there and some Perpendicular - a true statement of evolution and change over many centuries.

The Cathedral Interior

The architectural style used in the Cathedral is a mix of eleventh and twelfth century Norman, or Romanesque as it is also called, and medieval Gothic. For instance, in the nave the arcade, and the triforium, are both Norman, as is the external door on the south side of the western tower. The Norman style is epitomized by the round-headed arch and was very fashionable in the eleventh and twelfth centuries. In contrast the clerestory and the aisle windows are Early English Gothic from the thirteenth century, as is the three-light stepped eastern window.

The most spectacular internal feature is the Arundel Screen that separates the nave and choir. It is named after John Arundel who was bishop between 1458 and 1477. Built of stone it has three arches, the side ones being wider than that in the centre and there is a platform above that would have been used in the liturgy of certain special days.

The screen was removed in 1859 when attempts were made to open up the choir as a memorial to Dean Chandler. It was suggested at the time that the decision to remove the screen contributed to the problems that caused the tower and spire to collapse. The screen was stored in the northern transept till 1960 when it was re-erected in its original position.

In the south choir aisle there are two panels of Romanesque sculpture which were discovered in 1829. These date from the first half of the twelvth century and are considered to be particularly fine examples from that period; the two scenes record the visit of Jesus to Martha and Mary and the Raising of Lazarus.

In the south transept there are paintings by Lambert Barnard (1485-1567), court painter to Bishop Sherburne who was Bishop of Chichester in 1508-36. The two main scenes show St Wilfrid founding the see of Selsey in 681 and Bishop Sherburne asking Henry VIII to renew the charter. Around this there are oval medallions depicting James I, Charles I, Mary I, Elizabeth I and other monarchs.

St Richard of Chichester

Richard was Bishop of Chichester between 1245 and 1253 and his shrine is located within the Cathedral. This life-size-and-half statue was commissioned by the Friends of Chichester Cathedral to celebrate the Millennium. It is the work of Philip Jackson, it was unveiled by the Bishop and is located on the north-west approach to the Cathedral. Richard was born in 1197 and died in 1253. He was canonized in 1262. His shrine within the Cathedral became a major place of pilgrimage and was destroyed during the Reformation by the iconoclasts (in 1538) but re-established in 1930.

In 1987 the lower part of a man's arm was discovered in a reliquary during the restoration of the Abbey of La Lucerne in Normandy. The relic was thought to be Richard's and was moved to the Cathedral on 15 June 1990 and buried below the St Richard altar a year later. A further relic is kept in the Bishops' Chapel.

The modern St Richard's Shrine is located in the retro-quire and includes an altar designed by Jonathan Clarke, and the tapestry by Ursula Benker-Schirmer.

Richard's main contributions to the medieval Church was his requirement that all candidates for ordination should make a vow of chastity, a decree that married clergy should be deprived of their benefices and any concubines denied the privileges of the church. Rectors were expected to live in their parishes and vicars could only work in one parish. Richard placed great emphasis on the proper execution of clerical duties.

Bell Tower

Close by the north-west corner of the Cathedral is the bell tower whose origins probably date from after 1375 - and possibly as late as 1436. It was built to house the Cathedral bells and so avoid placing additional strains on the Cathedral tower which was built around this time.

Three grants towards the cost of building the tower are known to have been made in 1375, the early 1400s and around 1436. Certainly around 1428 Thomas Patching, the mayor, is supposed to have made a grant of 100 marks. The tower appears to have been built in stages. The heavy base with large set-back buttresses is in a style that suggests it was built in the fourteenth century, though the style of the south doorway suggests that it may have originated a little earlier and so may have been reset here, or perhaps suggests an earlier start date for the building.

Above there is an octagonal lantern with corner turrets and bell openings that seem to date from around 1440. Overall the clash of styles presents a strange contrast. Was the lantern added instead of a spire? Was it always intended to contrast so strongly? The tower houses eight bells, the oldest of which is from 1583. It also contains a clock.

The tower's survival is a rare example of the once common practice of housing the bells separately from the Cathedral to which they relate. Salisbury Cathedral had a similar bell tower which fell victim of Wyatt's radical renovations in the late 1700s and was demolished.

The Cloisters & the Chapel of St Faith

The building on the left – now the Education Centre – was the site of the Chapel of St Faith, and probably originated in the early thirteenth century. As early as around 1107 the feast of St Faith was selected as the date on which the Bishop's Sloe Fair would be held. The chapel was probably built to celebrate this linkage and a chantry was founded there in 1332.

However, by 1403 the chapel was in disrepair and this continued for much of the century, until eventually part of it was pulled down. It remained so until the late sixteenth century when it was converted into a dwelling.

Adjacent to the Education Centre is the eastern entrance to the cloisters. Chichester was always a secular establishment (that is it never housed a monastery) rather than a monastic one, and so the main purpose of the cloisters was to provide a covered passageway to the Cathedral from various residences on the south of the Cathedral. It was added in the fifteenth century when most of the other buildings already existed and this most probably explains its irregular shape.

The initial houses to accommodate the Bishop and principal members of the Cathedral staff were built around 1150 but burnt down in 1187 and then rebuilt. The Bishop's Palace, then as now, was to the west of the Cathedral with the Chancellor's house (since demolished) just north of it. The Treasurer's house was just to the west of St Richard's Lane which provided a route to the Cathedral for the Dean, Precentor and other canons who had houses in the aptly named Canon Lane which also provided a formal entrance to the Bishop's Palace. Extra prebends - canons who were financially independent of the Bishop but did not hold the major posts occupied by the residentiary canons - were appointed in the early sixteenth century and the Hall of Wiccamical Prebends was created for them on the south of the cloister next to the house for the Royal Chantry priests.

From early on it became common for many of the canons to be absent from the Cathedral and to employ vicars who would take their part in the services. Houses for them were created in Vicars' Close at the eastern end of the Close and this gave access to Vicars' Hall which was just outside the cloister.

Cathedral from St Richard's Walk

St Richard's Walk links the houses to the south of the Close - which were occupied by many of the clergy associated with the operation of the Cathedral - with the cloisters and the Cathedral. According to the *Buildings of England* it is 'sunny, comfortable, not too narrow', an epitome of Chichester and its Cathedral.

Behind the wall on the left is where the medieval Treasury was located. Today there is a house that was built by Canon Wagner in 1834-5 as a miniature of the vicarage he had erected for himself in Brighton.

The Wagner family had a varied career before it became enmeshed in Brighton religiosity. In the seventeenth century they were tailors in Silesia, in the eighteenth they were hatters in Pall Mall, cap-makers to the army, and outfitters to the gentry.

Henry Mitchell Wagner who built the house was born in 1792, the second and youngest son of Melchior Henry Wagner, hatter to George III and the army. H.M. Wagner became Vicar of Brighton in 1824, and throughout his incumbency - which lasted until his death in 1870 - he remained Vicar, and Brighton remained one Parish, being what has been called 'a Bishopric within a Bishopric'. H.M Wagner had one son, Arthur Douglas Wagner, who became perpetual curate of St Paul's in Brighton. He became infamous as a ritualist and for the Constance Kent case.

In 1860, when she was 16, Constance Kent murdered her half brother, who was aged under 4. She was arrested and discharged, as was the family governess. She joined St Mary's Home in Brighton in 1863, and while preparing for confirmation admitted the murder to Fr Wagner within the confessional. She gave herself up and was brought before a magistrate. She went for trial at Salisbury Assizes in 1865, pleaded guilty, was sentenced to death but had the sentence commuted to life imprisonment.

When Fr Wagner was called to give evidence he refused to reveal any information about what had transpired in the confessional. There was debate in Parliament about the right of a priest to remain silent and much agitation by the Protestant Association. Constance Kent remained in prison for 20 years (Millbank, Parkhurst, Woking and Fulham), then emigrated to Australia on her release where she changed her name to Ruth Emilie Kaye. She became a nurse and lived until 1944 when she was over 100. While in prison she made floor tiles, some of which are still preserved in Chichester.

Cathedral Spire from Refectory Garden

The first Cathedral spire was built sometime after the Cathedral, and probably around 1400. It has been suggested that those responsible had previously worked of the tower and spire at Salisbury.

In 1855 the London architect William Slater was appointed as consulting architect to the Cathedral. After the death of Dean Chandler in 1859, Slater was asked to make recommendations on how the Cathedral choir could be restored and enlarged as a memorial.

By May Slater had produced a report suggesting removal of the organ screen and the opening up of the choir, though by early 1860 he was questioning the safety of the proposals, and specifically whether the removal of the organ screen would endanger the stability of the building. A civil engineer - T. A. Yarrow - inspected the structure and concluded all was well.

In February the organ was partly removed, and the condition of part of the south-west pier was so bad that Yarrow was again asked to give his advice. He concluded that the defects did not pose a danger to the building. Work continued, and was inspected by another architect who also declared that there was no immediate danger.

Then on Wednesday 20 February 1861 a gale made 'the tower and spire to rock and to grind the stones together, and wherever there was a crack, pouring forth constant streams of dust'. Slater continued to supervise attempts to save the tower, but 'ominous cracking and superstitious noises' were heard, and at 1.25 pm the following day the spire and tower collapsed bringing down part of the Cathedral at the same time.

What we see today is a nineteenth-century tower and spire that was added in 1861-6 to replace those that had fallen in the gale.

George Bell House

Located between the entrance to the Bishop's Palace and the southern end of St Richard's Walk is George Bell House that was named after the Bishop of Chichester from 1929 to 1958.

Built of knapped flint with brick dressings and white timbering, the house is the result of a rebuilding of 1871. Inside a large hall and stairway act as a circulation focus for the substantial downstairs rooms and provide access to what is above.

Across the front façade are the words *Christus verum: Fundamentum + Sit huic Domo: Firmamentum* or *Christ the true foundation + May he be the strength of this house.*

Before the 1871 rebuilding, the earlier house was a residentiary and a college from 1839. The current elaborate Norman doorway may have been part of that earlier building or it may have been moved here in 1871. Either way it is a fine example of the Romanesque style with an inner order of zig-zags enclosing balls and more zig-zag around the outside.

As its dual names of Norman and Romanesque suggest, this was the style of architecture that became popular following the Norman Conquest and remained so during the eleventh and twelfth centuries. It was derived from the much earlier Roman style of architecture and perhaps was intended to symbolise the substance and elegance which the Normans brought with them – they were to be the new Romans.

Today the house is operated by the Cathedral authorities as a bed and breakfast centre which also hosts dinners and conferences.

Palace Gate

While the Cathedral represents the Bishop's seat of authority he is not responsible for the management of the Cathedral or its associated buildings. This task falls to the Dean and Chapter. As in many aspects of British life, power and authority are divided.

However, the Bishop's clerical seniority is recognised structurally in that his residence is referred to as a palace and it is the most substantial of all the Cathedral residences. The division of authority is also recognised structurally by the way the Bishop's Palace is approached through a large gateway which ensures that whoever passes through its archways is aware that they are moving into some inner sanctum.

The Palace Gate was erected in the fourteenth century, and, as Pevsner and Nairn so aptly puts it, was designed 'much more for use than for ornament'. It is built of rag stone with ashlar blocks for the buttresses that dominate the structure. There are two double-chamfered archways, one large for carriages and one much smaller for pedestrians. On the north side and above there is accommodation for a gate keeper.

SueFinniss

Bishop's Palace

By far the biggest and grandest building connected with the Cathedral is the Bishop's Palace which lies to the south-west and is approached from Canon Lane.

The plan is approximately a half H, with the cross-range running east/west and with side wings that project to the south.

The building has been rebuilt and modified numerous times so there is much doubt about the detail of its history and evolution.

There may be traces of a twelfth-century wall in the kitchen, though most of that part of the complex dates from the thirteenth century and may be the result of a rebuilding after a major fire in 1187.

Much of the cross-range may be slightly earlier - late twelfth or early thirteenth-century.

The western wing most probably dates from the fifteenth or early sixteenth centuries, and much of the whole structure was changed at this time as part of a major rebuilding programme. The long eastern wing that connects with the gatehouse was most probably also built at this time.

Vicars' Close

Vicars were paid clergy who deputised for absent canons. The size of the original Vicars' Close shows just how extensive the practice was.

The residences in Vicars' Close were originally on both sides of a rectangular enclosure, though only those on the west have survived along with one on the east. The remainder were converted into shops with access to South Street. The front walls of the residences are from the fifteenth century, the remainder being much altered and rebuilt in the eighteenth century.

The Vicars' Close gave way to the Vicars' Hall which itself opened out on the north close to the cloister. The Vicars' Hall is mostly from the fourteenth and fifteenth centuries, though with late twelfth-century elements in the undercroft. There was a hall, a parlour and dormitories.

Clearly being a canon was a prestigious and well rewarded position, but there were more attractive options elsewhere which caused many to entrust their Cathedral responsibilities to a less wealthy ordained minister who would perform the duties in exchange for accommodation and some income.

Today the Vicars' Close provides a pleasant retreat from the busyness of the Cathedral and city.

Canon Gate

Unlike Salisbury, Chichester Cathedral and its associated buildings are not separated from the city by a wall although it has an elegant gateway on the east which marks the entry and exit point to South Street.

The date of its original construction is uncertain but is probably not earlier than the sixteenth century.

A large arch provided access for carriages while there is a much smaller one for pedestrians on the south side. Above the arches there is accommodation. The building fell into disrepair and was restored, the upper storey being rebuilt by the architect Ewan Christian in 1894.

There are niches in the upper storey both inside and outside the Close and both were decorated with the letters IHS (now indistinct through erosion), a well used Christian symbol based on the first three letters of Jesus in Greek.

The western niche also contained the coat of arms of William of Wykeham (c.1320-1404) who was Bishop of Winchester, founder of Winchester College, New College, Oxford, and the Chancellor of England.

Sue Finniss

This gargoyle is on the south side of the cathedral. It was carved by Joslins Stonemasonry of Oxford in the 1990s. It represents a solicitor, and previous Chapter Clerk, named Clifford Hodges.

The City

Market Cross

The Market Cross was erected in 1501 by Edward Story (Bishop of Chichester 1478-1503) and endowed in his will with £25 a year to cover its upkeep. John Britton described it as 'the most enriched and beautiful example of its class in England'.

At this time the visual effect of the Market Cross would have been much greater as it was placed in the centre of a much larger square which marked the joining point of North, South, East and West streets. Further building at the junction of these streets has now greatly reduced the size of the square and the visual impact of the Market Cross.

Markets were always important to Chichester as they acted as an economic focus for those who lived in the surrounding area, and for a thriving corn and cattle trade. Certainly from the twelfth century, and most probably earlier, there were markets on Wednesdays and Saturdays with one on Friday being added somewhat later. The Market Cross would have provided the central focus for such activities and acted as a counter balance to the adjacent Cathedral. It marked the growth of a secular economic power.

After 1808 the Cross ceased to be so important when the Market House was opened in North Street and the Market Cross was railed in. The railings were removed in 1872.

The structure is octagonal with a central supporting column, elegant stone ribs and large buttresses. The whole is topped with finials and a lantern and decorated with a bronze of Charles I and clocks to help regulate the lives of the inhabitants. The clocks was added in 1724 and the lantern modified in 1746.

All Saints in the Pallant, West Pallant

Located on the north side of West Pallant, this early thirteenth-century, deconsecrated Anglican church is now home to Agora Asset Management.

Before deconsecration the plan was very simple with a rectangular structure subdivided between a large nave and a much smaller chancel that was slightly elevated, but not distinguished structurally in any other way. A small vestry was added on the north-eastern side during the nineteenth century.

Typical of humble churches in this area. the walls are of knapped flint with stone dressings and some rendering. Light is provided through simple lancet windows. The roofs are tiled and there is a sturdy single bell-cote at the western end. Its bell would have called the faithful to worship but also marked out the religious divisions of the day.

45

West Pallant

The district of Pallant is east of South Street and south of East Street. It was divided into four sections by streets named North, South, East and West Pallant. A Market Cross stood at the meeting point of these four streets, opposite Pallant House. It was demolished in 1713.

In the eighteenth century this was a residential area, and most of the houses were either rebuilt or re-fronted in the Georgian style during the eighteenth century. The Pallants were where the professional classes lived in the eighteenth and nineteenth centuries. This view looks west towards the Cathedral from the junction of North, South, East and West Pallant.

Pallant Court, number 10, is on the left with the brick built number 5 on the right along with the cream coloured numbers 3-4.

Number 5 is an impressive Georgian town house which was built in the 1760s to replace two earlier houses. It has five bays, the central three of which project slightly, and is topped by a pediment above the second floor.

Initially it was owned by the Sanden family and its most famous eighteenth-century occupant was Dame Agnes Frankland, a poor American who achieved notoriety when she married the wealthy Sir Harry Frankland.

In 1817 it was described as having 'eating, drawing and breakfast rooms' on the ground floor and four bed chambers above plus attics above that and a basement below.

Pallant House

A wonderful example of the sort of house which would have been occupied by the better off in the eighteenth century, and of the Georgian style of architecture, is Pallant House that is on the east side of the North Pallant.

The house is sometimes known as the Dodo House because of the ostriches on the top of the gate piers and was built around 1712 by Henry Peckham (1683-1764). It was one of the first brick houses to be built in the city in the eighteenth century and replaced an earlier structure. It is perhaps the best Georgian building in Chichester.

Henry Peckham was a wealthy wine merchant and was known as 'Lisbon' Peckham because of his involvement with the Portuguese wine trade. His grandfather was Recorder of Chichester under Charles II.

The entrance and ground floor are elevated above the street and approached by elegant steps that are emphasised by the gate piers topped by the ostriches. The main façade is built of brick and of seven bays, the central three of which are brought forward and marked by brick quoins. The central doorway is surrounded by an elaborate door case decorated with Corinthian pilasters.

The first floor is equally elegant and topped by a stone parapet that partly hides the roof, though not the great square chimneys that dominate each end of the building. The extension at the north west end of the roof was added later. There is also a basement.

By the middle of the nineteenth century, William Duke, who was a solicitor, occupied the house. It was acquired by Westhampnett Rural District Council in 1916, was restored in 1979 and became part of what is now Pallant House Gallery in 1982.

St John the Evangelist, St John's Street

During the eighteenth century the Church of England's liturgy centred on Bible reading and sermons, with communion being a less regular occurrence. Then in the early part of the nineteenth century there was a revival of interest in the older, more sacramental, forms of worship, which emerged from the debates of what became known as the Oxford Movement during the 1830s and 1840s. Here the emphasis was on the eucharist and baptism and the architectural emphasis on Gothic. The altar became the most dominant feature, and it was usually elevated at the eastern end. What was St Peter the Great in West Street, is an excellent example of the sort of church that emerged from these developments.

However, St John the Evangelist is an example of the earlier form of worship which placed great emphasis upon the pulpit. It also evidences a privately funded form of Anglicanism that created what were known as proprietary chapels. These were seen as a way of providing religion for the growing urban population through private enterprise. St John's was built in 1812-13.

By 1813 there were 18 shareholders who had invested a total of £3,200 and also a long list of donors. In March that year the sale of pews commenced.

In the gallery there were 54 enclosed pews, each of which would hold several people. The rents varied between £2/16/- and £11/14/- per year depending upon size and position. Downstairs there were 33 servants' seats along the north and south walls, 38 enclosed pews and free benches for the poor. The pew rents varied between £2/2/- and £8/1/-.

The project was estimated to produce pew rents of about £500 a year, that interest on the shares would amount to £160, the Minister would be paid £120 and other costs would amount to £50 leaving a surplus of about £330. The interior was reorganized in 1879 and the free seats seem to have disappeared at this stage.

The church is dominated by a triple-decker pulpit. The churchwarden would read the notices from the bottom position, the Bible would be read from the middle level and the sermon delivered from the top. Just like in a theatre today the best seats attracted the highest charges. The separate staircases made sure that the rich and poor did not have to mingle. The chancel and altar are insignificant features that were only used for high feasts and even then only a minority of the congregation would take communion. St John's is now owned by the Churches Conservation Trust.

SueFinniss

Corn Exchange

Corn was always important to Chichester, which acted as a commercial centre for the surrounding area and its agricultural produce.

Originally there was a Corn Exchange on the west side of North Street but this was replaced by the grand building in East Street that now houses a Next retail outlet.

It was built in 1831-2 to the designs of John Elliott, a Southampton architect, and has a giant fluted, Greek Doric portico, with a plain pediment above. The portico straddles the pavement while the business part of the building stretches out behind. Its elegant grandeur proclaims the importance of the trade in corn and its impact on the local economy.

However, things change quickly and by the late 1800s the Corn Exchange had become the Exchange Cinema, and then later the Granada Cinema. In 1896 it was where the first moving picture show took place in Chichester. In 1967 the rear of the building was converted into offices, and when the cinema closed around 1983, the front was converted into a McDonalds before being adapted again to its current use.

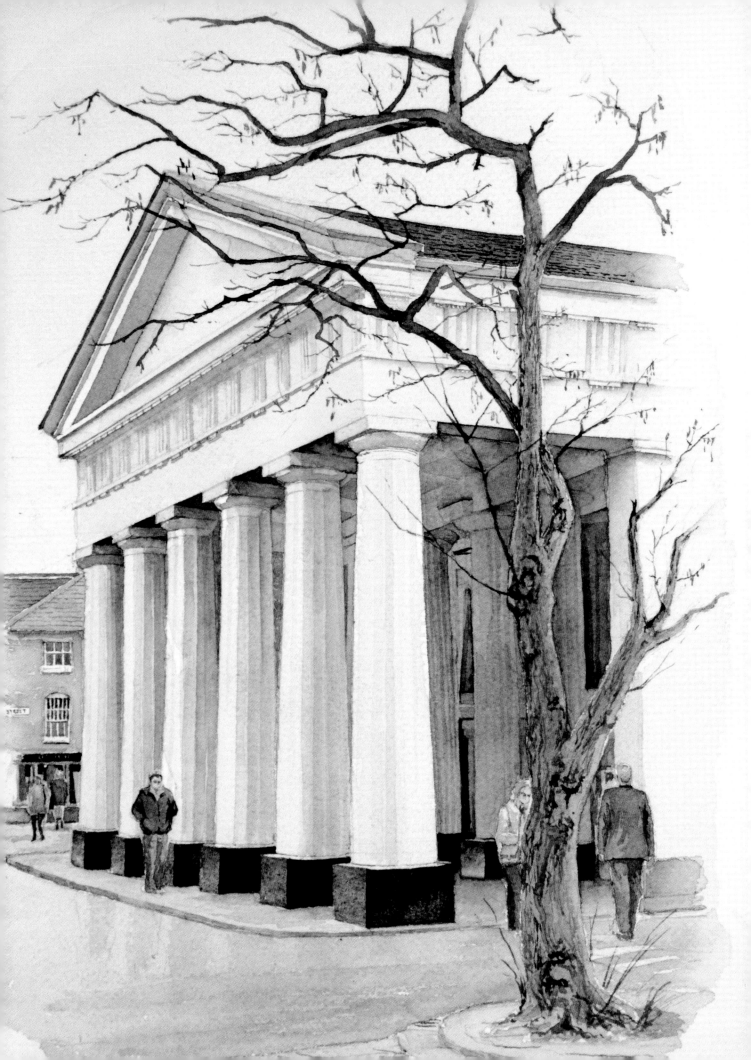

St Andrew, Oxmarket

One of the earliest churches in Chichester, St Andrew's dates from the thirteenth century with window tracery added in the fourteenth and fifteenth centuries. The earliest documentary evidence is dated 1248.

It was a single-cell church with the altar at the eastern end, and would have served the north-east section of the city. It is roughcast on the exterior but with some medieval relief panels still showing in the walls.

Prior to recent changes to create a car park at the rear of the building, this church would have been tucked away out of sight and only accessible down the narrow passageway from East Street.

There were plans to add a north aisle and vestry and to create an enlarged sanctuary and choir in the mid nineteenth century, though there was much opposition and the plans failed. A decorative bell turret was added around this time.

In the Reformation period the church seems to have been associated with Catholic recusancy and this association was reinforced when Henry Manning, then Archdeacon of Chichester, preached there in 1849. Manning later went on to become a cardinal in the Roman Catholic Church.

The church was made redundant in the 1950s and in 1969 much of the churchyard was paved. The idea of an Arts Centre originated in the 1960s, was given impetus in 1972 and restoration was completed by June 1976 when St Andrew's opened as the Chichester Centre of Art.

The Dolphin & Anchor

On the north of West Street, opposite the Cathedral, was the site of two of Chichester's main coaching inns – The Dolphin and The Anchor – which competed for many years before merging in the twentieth century.

The Dolphin was an inn by 1666 while The Anchor, which forms the westerly part of the group of buildings, and is separated by a small shop from The Dolphin, was an inn from at least 1737. They were not merged into a single establishment until 1910 when they were acquired by Trust Houses Ltd.

The current facade dates from the late eighteenth century – probably 1768, though much enlarged in 1791 - and presents a fine modern, Georgian façade as a contrast to the medieval Cathedral opposite.

The Dolphin was a coaching-inn, and it was from here that the coaches for London and the south coast destinations departed. In 1786 a coach left for Brighton on Monday, Wednesday and Friday and returned the following day. These connected with coaches to Portsmouth, Southampton and the west of England. The fare to Brighton was 10/-. In 1792 a daily coach departed to Holborn and from 1803 there were daily coaches to Charing Cross and Fleet Street. It was here that the coaches would have stopped, horses would have been changed, meals served and overnight accommodation provided. In many ways it was both a centre for transport and a civic hub; somewhere you met and dined with visitors.

Later, in 1846, the railway came to Chichester in the form of a south coast extension to the London to Brighton line, and the train provided a much faster and more comfortable means of getting to London and the days of the coaching inn were coming to an end.

The three-storey, six-bay building which was The Anchor, now houses The Dolphin & Anchor pub. Then there is a simple two-bay building before we get to the grander eight-bay structure that is mostly now home to Waterstones. There is a grand entrance doorway that gave access to an assembly room on the first floor which was built by Abel Smith as a meeting place for Liberal supporters, and evidences the wider use that the building served. The mews entrance would have given access to the stables. The Anchor was the Tory meeting place.

St Peter the Great (now Wests Bar), West Street

In 1847 the parish church of Chichester was located in the north transept of the Cathedral, an arrangement which, according to the Cathedral Restoration Committee, made the transept 'not only unsightly and sordid in its actual condition, but ... [one which was] incapable under any circumstances of being made a suitable place for Worship for its large Parish'. A thorough restoration of the Cathedral was planned, and the Committee decided that a part of this process should include the building of a separate parish church.

In November 1847 Richard Cromwell Carpenter, a London based architect who was also designing the Woodard schools at Lancing, Ardingly and Hurstpierpoint, presented his designs for a church to hold 700. In January 1848 work started by demolishing the existing buildings and clearing the site, and the foundation stone was laid on 17 August. By January 1850 the walls and roof were complete, the church being 'secure from the weather', though shortage of funds had caused some prevarication over the projected tower. Finally the idea of a tower was dropped, and priority given to funding restoration work in the Cathedral. The church was consecrated on 1 July 1852, when the total cost had risen to £5,450/8/5d.

The result was a sizable church of ashlar Caen stone, which had been modelled on the design used for the medieval Austin Friars' church in London. It attracted enthusiastic reviews and has been described as 'one of the best of its kind that we have seen. There is a graciousness about it that is often entirely missing from Victorian churches. The outside will one day be indistinguishable from a 14th century church: the inside is more definitely Victorian – but good Victorian'.

Sadly religious decline has meant a new use and after a spell as an antique centre, the church now houses Wests Bar. The founders would have shuddered!

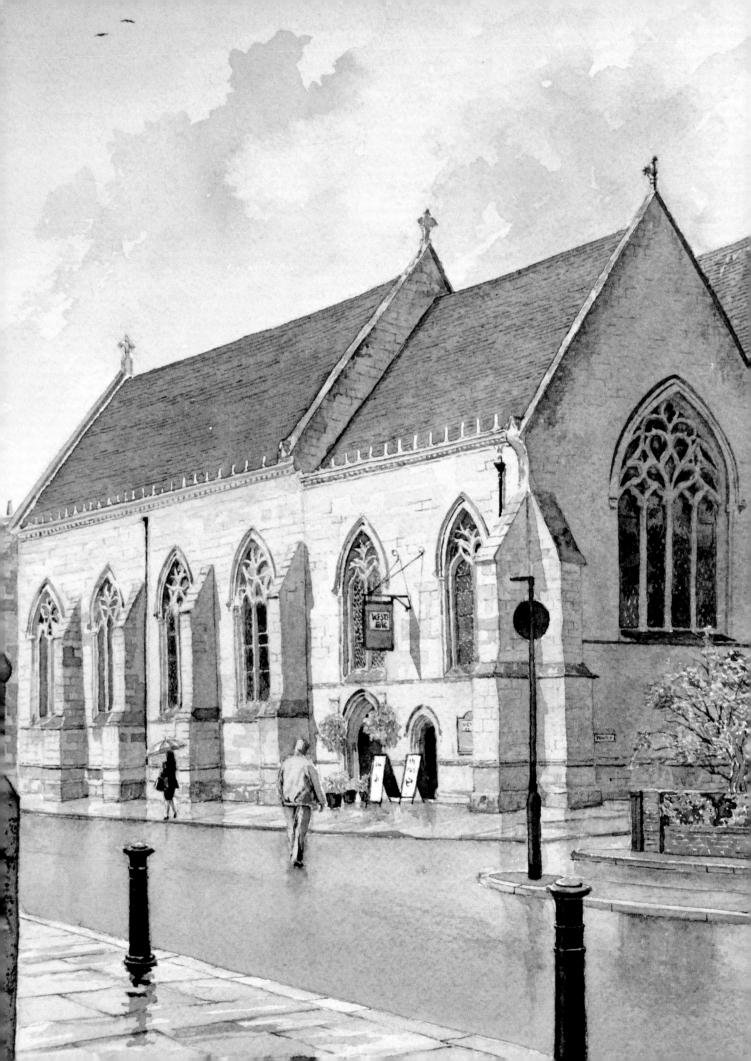

Ede's House

This was one of the first Georgian-style houses to be built in the city and originates from 1696. It is constructed of brick with stone dressings, has seven bays, the central three of which are slightly recessed. Above there are hipped roofs and below a basement.

The house was occupied for a time in the eighteenth century by the Rev. Thomas D'Oyly, who was Chancellor of the Cathedral from 1747 until 1770. Sir Arthur Fairbairn lived there between 1909-14 when it became a centre of high culture. It was acquired by the County Council in 1916 and used as the principal council office until 1936 when the County Hall was built.

The house was nameless until 1841 when it started to be known as Westgate House. Then in 1905 it changed to West House, and it changed again in 1911 when it became Wren's House after Sir Christopher Wren, though there is no evidence to suggest that he had anything to do with its design. In 1967 it became the County Record Office and was renamed Ede's House after John Ede, a local maltster.

The house was separated from the roadway by red-brick walls and a wrought iron gateway whose pillars were topped by urns and pineapples.

Market House, North Street

This is a further example of how Chichester acted as a market focus for the surrounding area and its agricultural produce.

In 1802 it was decided that holding markets in different parts of the city was far from ideal and that a single market should be built. In 1804 the scheme was temporarily abandoned because of the cost, and it was not until 1806 that it was decided to go ahead.

A site was bought for £650 and further land added later. The development was authorized by an Act of Parliament in 1808.

The Market House was built in 1807-8 at a contract price of £1,522 and opened for business on 20 January 1808. The designs were produced by the nationally important John Nash (1752-1835), who had royal patronage and was one of the most influential architects of his period. In London he later had a hand in the remodelling of the Royal Opera House in 1816-18, designed the Haymarket Theatre in 1820-1, All Souls, church in Langham Place (currently used by the BBC) in 1822-5, and worked on Buckingham Palace and Clarence House. He was a favourite of the aristocracy, and his presence in Chichester says a lot about its rise to prominence at the start of the nineteenth century.

As with most Classical buildings the impact is where everyone can see it. The street frontage that is dominated by a Doric colonnade topped by an entablature, a balustrade, and the city arms. There was an open fish market at the rear, and seven shops, or stalls, down each side in front of this. The top storey with Ionic pilasters was an extension of about 1900.

The Market House became an art annex to Chichester College and is now called the Buttermarket and is home to a number of retail outlets.

Sue Furniss

St Olave's Church, North Street

This is the oldest church in Chichester. The nave walls appear to be early Norman, suggesting that the Normans started building a permanent settlement in Chichester soon after their arrival.

The chancel area is from the thirteenth century and replaced an earlier, and shorter structure. It has been much restored in later periods and especially in 1851. The western end, which fronts North Street, is of knapped flint and probably from about 1400.

It therefore seens that the building of St Olave's would have started about the same time as work on the Cathedral and perhaps provided a place for worship while work on the larger building progressed. In time no doubt, St Olave's would have become a church for the city dwellers.

Today it is a bookshop.

Council House & Assembly Rooms

In the early 1700s a Market House existed near this site; probably a few yards to the south of the current building. It was timber-framed and stood on stilts. There was a council chamber above and open space beneath where the market stalls were erected.

Then in 1728-9 the decision was made to create a new building which better reflected the rising importance of the city, and, at a cost of £280, a site was acquired where a Roman temple to Neptune and Minerva had once stood.

At the behest of the Duke of Richmond, the designer Lord Burlington (1694-1753) produced designs that were drawn up by Henry Flitcroft (1697-1769) - architecturally both were nationally important. The plan was for a narrow building with three bays facing North Street and twelve bays behind. It was rejected, most probably because it was too large and expensive. Burlington then produced a second, less ornate, scheme. The front façade was widened by the addition of two flanking wings and a semi-circular apse was created at the eastern end. This design was also rejected.

The council turned to Roger Morris who designed the front part of what is there today. His plans were approved in 1730 and the building erected in 1731- 3 at a cost of £1,271.

The style is Palladian - Ionic columns support an entablature with lower flanking wings which tend to emphasize the centre of the façade. There is a very elegant Palladian Council Chamber upstairs which has a decorative Doric cornice. The ground floor was open.

It may have suited the good people of Chichester but Nikolas Pevsner and Ian Nairn were less complimentary, describing it as a 'perfect example of Palladian ideas applied by a man who did not know what on earth to do with them'. This criticism is perhaps more than a little unkind as Morris (1695-1749) was a highly respected and prolific London-based architect who was much used by the landed gentry.

An Assembly Room was added at the rear in 1781-3. The designs were produced by James Wyatt (1746-1813), another prominent national architect, although the result was very utilitarian in comparison to the grandeur of the Council Chamber. The buiding was extended again in 1830 when Courts of Justice were added to the south and these were later converted into another assembly room.

Greyfriars or Guildhall

In the thirteenth century the Franciscan Friary was relocated to, what is today, Prior Park and around 1269 work started on the construction of a large Friary church, cloisters and domestic buildings.

What remains today was the chancel of a much larger structure that probably included a substantial central tower and a very large nave with aisles. The chancel was built in 1279-80.

The complex remained under the Friars until the monasteries were dissolved in 1538, and three years later the site was given to the mayor who promptly sold it to the City Corporation.

In 1541 the chancel was converted for secular use and became a Guildhall and an Assize. The central tower and nave, cloisters and other buildings may have been demolished at this stage or slightly earlier. It remained as an Assize until 1748, was the town hall until 1850 and was involved in the election process until 1888. William Blake was tried there in 1804 when he was charged with assault, and with uttering seditious and treasonable expressions against the king. He is alleged to have shouted 'Damn the king. The soldiers are all slaves.' He was acquitted.

By 1850 the Sussex Rifle Volunteers had started to use the building as an armoury and drill hall. It then stood empty from the early twentieth century until 1947 when it became a museum.

The building is of knapped flint dressed with Binstead and Caen stone and built in an Early English Gothic style. There are 5 bays plus a half bay at the western end. The sides are pierced by simple 2-light lancets topped by 4-foils while the eastern end has a fine 5-light stepped arrangement of lancets which probably dates from the late thirteenth century.

St Mary's Hospital

The hospital was probably founded in 1158 on a site at the junction of South and East Streets, near the Market Cross. It was when the Grey Friars moved from the current hospital site to Priory Park around 1253 that work started in earnest on the creation of what now is St Mary's Hospital. The building was completed around 1292.

Medieval hospitals saw little distinction between curing the body and the soul, patients in need of care – the poor and the sick – were accommodated in a building that placed them close to, and hopefully in sight of, the chapel.

Here the main building resembled a church with the patients accommodated in the nave and the chapel occupying what would have been the chancel. In the seventeenth century, when religious fervour was less enthusiastic, and the desire for individualism more assertive, the patients' part of the complex was divided into self-contained units.

The original main building was slightly longer – it was later shortened by one bay. Originally it was an aisled hall that was built of flint walls and timber framing which creates six large bays and a kingpost structure that supported an enormous tiled roof that is now pierced by chimneystacks of 1680. The stone chapel is at the eastern end and contains an oak screen from about 1300, and 24 misericord stalls which are earlier than those in the Cathedral.

Four adjacent cottages were converted into almshouses in 1905, St Mary's Lodge was added in 1986 and St Mary's Courtyard in 2003.

The hospital continues to serve the same purpose as it was built to provide in the thirteenth century, and is home to 30 residents, cared for by a staff team and chaplain.

St Martin's Square

Another fine Georgian-style house, this time in St Martin's Square in the north eastern quarter of the city. This is number 20 which was built in 1758 on land that was leased to a James Nountsher.

The house is of red brick, with two storeys and three bays, the most elegant of which is that in the centre which protrudes forward, has an Greek Doric doorcase with a Venetian window and a brick pediment above.

This, and in houses like it, is where the fashionable would have lived. The house was modern and conveniently located to enable the occupants to participate fully in the life of the city in an age before the motor car widened personal mobility.

Chichester Festival Theatre

Leslie Evershed-Martin, a local ophthalmic optician and former mayor, provided the inspiration and leadership that led to the Festival Theatre being built. This happened after he had become fascinated by a BBC TV programme *Monitor* on the Shakespeare Festival Theatre in Stratford, Ontario.

The Canadian town was about the same size as Chichester and they had started holding a summer theatre festival there in 1953 with a tent which was erected over a thrust stage. The thrust stage projected forwards into the audience - it is an arrangement based on ancient Greek and Roman theatres. A permanent structure followed in 1957 and still operates today.

Evershed-Martin motivated people in Chichester to replicate the development, and a site in Oaklands Park was selected. The architectural firm of Powell & Moya were appointed – they had designed the Skylon for the 1951 Festival of Britain. Philip Powell's father was a canon in the Cathedral.

The design was rather similar to that used in Canada and was dominated by the thrust stage. The structure was hexagonal and built of reinforced concrete.

H.R.H Princess Alexandra of Kent laid the foundation stone on 12 May 1961 and the building was completed by 3 May 1962. Like the Canadian theatre, it was designed just for summer use, so there was a shortage of dressing rooms and other facilities that were compensated for by erecting tents in the adjoining park. At that time Chichester had the only modern thrust stage in the UK. Laurence Olivier was appointed as the first Artistic Director and the initial production followed on 5 July was *The Chances* by John Fletcher.

An extension followed in 1967 and others have been added since. Over the 50 years since its inception the Chichester Festival Theatre has developed from a summer festival venue to a critically acclaimed award-winning theatre of national standing.

However, the years have taken their toll and many of the physical and technical aspects of the theatre are now outdated. So in 2010 Haworth Tomkins were asked to undertake a conservation management study and a feasibility study followed. Plans have now been produced to revamp and extend the building so that it can continue to provide cutting-edge theatre in the coming decades. Planning approval has been sought and obtained and an application made for an Arts Council grant.

The adjacent Minerva Theatre arose after the Festival Theatre became more established and a demand grew for impromptu performances. A tented theatre was created opposite the Festival Theatre. The desire for a more permanent home led to the current theatre being built and opened in April 1989.

Out & Around

Chichester's Canal

Despite being at the head of Chichester Harbour the centre of Chichester is still a few miles from navigable water. In an age before the railways and roads transformed internal communications, water was still the best means of transporting goods and access to it provided a real commercial advantage. London was a major trading centre, as were the south coast centres of Southampton and Portsmouth. However, getting from one to the other was not as simple as it appeared. To travel by ship down the Thames and then around Kent and through the Straits of Dover was a reasonably hazardous business so an inland canal was always an attractive option once canal building technology had been developed.

For Chichester this meant an inland route from London to Portsmouth which used the Thames, Wey and Chichester Harbour, all of which would be connected by new canals. The resulting Portsmouth and Arundel Canal was engineered by John Rennie and the final section opened in 1823.

To complete the linkage between London and Portsmouth the waterway at Ford near Arundel, was linked to Birdham on Chichester Harbour, by a new 12 mile stretch of canal which opened in 1823 after 5 years of construction effort.

There had long been a desire to link Chichester with the harbour and there was a proposal made as early as 1585 to create a link to Dell Quay. Further plans followed in the early 1800s. So Chichester did not want to be left out of this development and plans were created to link a basin just south of the city centre with the canal at Hunston, and in the process create a link between Chichester and the sea, but also a means of moving agricultural materials between farms and of draining the surrounding countryside.

Approval was granted in 1817, construction started in 1818 and the spur was opened in 1822, a year ahead of the main canal. The scale of the spur was such that it was intended to accommodate vessels up to 85' long and 18' beam.

In reality the canal made its appearance on the scene too late and was soon challenged by the railways which offered a far quicker and more efficient alternative. Traffic dwindled and it soon failed economically. Traffic on the spur was better than across the whole Portsmouth and Arundel Canal, though even that struggled and the canal closed to traffic in 1906.

Today the canal still exists, though navigation is restricted because of low road bridges and stop-planked locks.

Sue Finniss

Holy Trinity, Bosham

Bosham is located just a few miles from Chichester on a small peninsula between two tidal creeks at the north-eastern part of Chichester harbour. People have lived here, and at nearby Fishbourne, since Roman times, and the Romans may have constructed the village's mill-stream. It is also suggested that they built a basilica here.

A church at Bosham is the earliest documented reference to a Christian church in Sussex. The Venerable Bede mentions Bosham in *The Ecclesiastical History of the English Nation*, and cites St Wilfrid's visit here around 681 when he discovered a small monastery.

Tradition has it that Canute lived here, and Bosham is one of only five places that appear on the map attached to the Anglo-Saxon Chronicle. Harold sailed from here in 1064 and as a consequence Bosham is mentioned by name on the Bayeux Tapestry which refers to the meeting of Harold and Edward the Confessor on the way to meet William of Normandy to discuss who would succeed Edward to the throne. The Domesday Book (1086) lists Bosham as one of the wealthiest manors in England.

Around 850 a church was built, although nothing now remains of that building. The lower three stages of the tower of the present church date from the eleventh century, the belfry above coming slightly later (*c.* 1080–1110). Parts of the chancel were built in the eleventh century, the north aisle was added in the twelfth, then the chancel was extended eastwards in the early thirteenth and the south aisle added in the fourteenth. Much was heavily restored by the Victorians in the nineteenth century.

Sue Furniss

Sailing in Chichester Harbour

Chichester Harbour is home to 17 sailing clubs. Perhaps the most prestigious is the Hayling Island Sailing Club that is located at the entrance to Chichester Harbour. This attracts sailors from most of the national squads because of the strong tidal streams that provide a real challenge to even the best sailors.

The remaining sailing clubs are located throughout the harbour and trypical is that at Bosham which was founded in 1907. and held its first regatta the following year. The club aims to provide the opportunity for members of all ages to enjoy the sea, to develop their skills in sailing and racing, to participate in social events, and to create and maintain friendships in a congenial environment.

It was not untill 1955 that the club acquired a lease on Mill House - which is depicted here - from the Earl of Iveagh who was Lord of the Manor of Bosham, and it was converted to become the clubhouse and replace other temporary accommodation that had previously been used. Later the club also aqquired the adjacent cottage and the two buildings were merged to produce what exists today.

In its early days the club also operated from Cobnor and Itchenor. In 1927-8 Itchenor Sailing Club was formed as a separate institution, and in 1972 a pavilion was erected at Cobnor so as to make the facilities more permanent and to relieve any pressure on the slipway at Bosham.

In 1992 the club became a limited company and made major structural changes to the clubhouse.

Today Bosham Sailing Club is a thriving organization.

Roman Palace, Fishbourne

The Romans invaded Britain in 43AD and established a bridgehead at Richborough in Kent. They advanced across Kent and crossed the Thames before heading north-east and establishing a major settlement at Colchester. A second front was opened to Fishbourne, and this became the base from which the Isle of Wight was conquered along with the south coast as far as Topsham on the river Exe.

The palace at Fishbourne would have been an immense complex, begun around 75AD and taking about five years to build. It was designed to a Mediterranean plan with four ranges gathered around a central garden, the south range then fronting Chichester Harbour. Elegant mosaics decorated the rooms which numbered about 100, and the settlement was clearly used by a Roman officer of some considerable stature. This was a display of elegance which would have been unknown in Britain at that time; a real statement of power through architecture.

The west wing was destroyed by fire between 270AD and 280AD and the palace was then vacated, demolished and the stone re-used elsewhere. In 1960 Roman fragments were discovered during construction of a water main and a wider area was then excavated by local amateur archaeologists. Faced with the threat that the site could be sold for building development, the current complex, which contains the remains of the north range of the original palace, was acquired by Ivan Margary, a prominent local archaeologist. Much of the remainder of the site is buried below the A27 and a housing development.

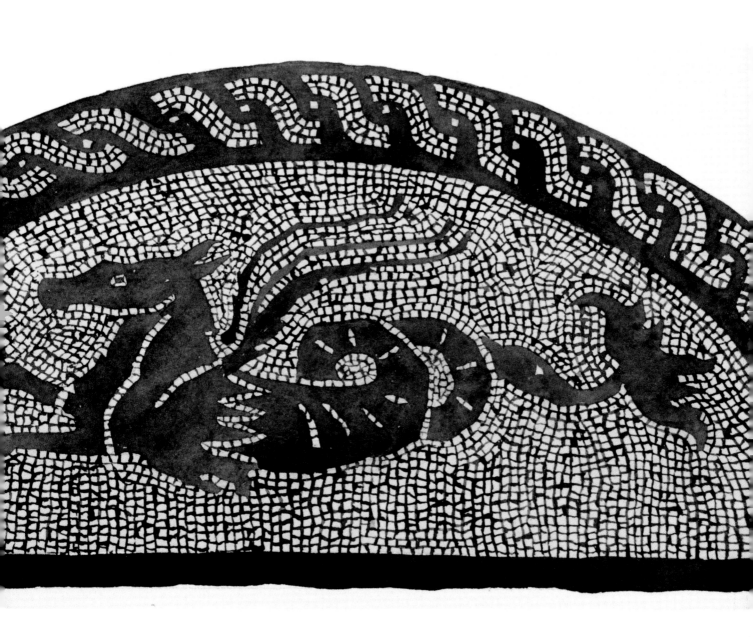

West Dean

Originally a medieval house stood here but was replaced by a Jacobean one in 1622. This structure was then engulfed within a further new building which was designed by James Wyatt in 1804-8 for the politician Sir James Peachey. Its architecture was intended to create the impression that the house had been built in stages over many years and was a product of evolution and growth rather than some new assertive statement of a new age. It was about 300 feet long and faced with knapped flint.

Then in 1891 the house and surrounding estate were bought for £200,000 by William Dodge James (1854-1912) and his new wife Evelyn, née Forbes. James was heir to two American fortunes which had been amassed from the railways and metal-broking. He wanted to live the life of the country gentleman while his wife was an amateur actress and a captivating socialist who was accepted in royal circles. King Edward VII and Queen Alexandra were regular visitors and so West Dean had to be transformed into a venue for lavish and massive entertaining.

The task fell to Ernest George, one of the leading early twentieth-century architects (initially in partnership with Harold Peto and then later with Alfred Yeates). All the internal spaces were remodelled, replanned and redecorated and the hall made into a major feature which recalled the medieval era in a romantic way. A new service wing was built along with another that had additional reception rooms and bedrooms. In 1905 the prominent porte-cochère was added.

The house subsequently passed to Edward James who feared that a consequence of WWII would be that the techniques of the craftsmen would be lost and so he set about establishing an educational trust that would foster craftsmanship.

Despite this aim, a girls' boarding school occupied the building from 1956 until 1968 when it assumed its current use as a college devoted to the study of conservation and the visual arts.

West Dean Gardens

Part of the Edwardian dream was an extensive garden, but not one dominated exclusively by plants and vegetation. The garden was to be a constructed affair with large elements of hard landscaping that provided the backdrop and framework on which the plants could display their beauty while also providing a series of passageways which would be used to convey the human observers through this constructed paradise.

One of the pioneers of this form of gardening was the partnership between Edwin Lutyens and Gertrude Jekyll. The garden at West Dean is a further development of that genre and one where the pergola is a major feature.

Harold Peto was responsible for the garden design between 1905 and 1909 and he used the language of Classical architecture to express his ideas. It was here that the guests would wander on bright, sunny days. In effect the garden became an extension of the house - a series of outside rooms.

Chichester Harbour

Chichester Harbour is a Site of Special Scientific Interest, and a European Special Protection Area because of its importance for wildlife. It has the sixth largest saltmarsh area in Britain, supports about 50,000 wintering and migrating birds each year, and its marshes support a number of scarce plant species.

The Chichester Harbour Trust and the Friends of Chichester Harbour both attempt to protect this rich heritage while recognizing that the harbour is located in a heavily populated and prosperous part of the UK which generates a strong demand for leisure facilities.

There is evidence that the harbour was settled in the Neolithic and Iron Age periods, while in the Roman era it also assumed a military importance that was focused on Fishbourne. Dell Quay and Bosham became significant ports, and in the thirteenth century Emsworth also became a port. Fishing and oyster dredging were both important until the twentieth century.

Because of the large expanse of protected water, Chichester Harbour is home to a number of sailing clubs. Much dinghy sailing takes place within the harbour and a large number of cruisers anchor in its protected waters before venturing out into the English Channel.

This painting shows Emsworth and looks from the eastern part of the town towards the sailing clubs. Emsworth was originally a Saxon settlement before developing into a busy port with ship and boat building, rope making, brewing and had tidal grain mills.

Bibliography

Barry Cunliffe, *Fishbourne* (Sussex Archaeological Society, 1977)

Alan H.J. Green, *The Buildings of Georgian Chichester 1690-1830* (Phillimore, 2007)

Alan H. J. Green, *The History of Chichester's Canal* (Sussex Industrial Archaeology Society, 2009)

Ken Green, *Chichester: An Illustrated History* (Breedon Books, 2011)

Mary Hobbs (ed.), *Chichester Cathedral: An Historical Survey* (Phillimore, 1994)

Ian Nairn & Nikolaus Pevsner, *The Buildings of England: Sussex* (Penguin, 1965)

L.F. Salzman (ed.), *The Victoria History of the Counties of England: A History of Sussex* (vol III) (Oxford University Press, 1935)

Some useful dates

43	Romans arrived
75	Building of Fishbourne Palace commenced
c.270-280	Fishbourne Palace damaged by fire and deserted
681	Bishopric created at Selsey
878-9	Fortified town created by Alfred the Great
1064	Harold supposedly sailed from Bosham
1075	Bishopric moved to Chichester
1076-87	Work starts on building of Norman Cathedral
1091	Building recommences after short break
1104	City fortified and castle built
1108	Cathedral dedicated
1114	City and Cathedral damaged by fire
1125	Rebuilding of Cathedral complete
1158	St Mary's Hospital founded in centre of city
1184	Cathedral consecrated
1187	Fire damages Cathedral again
1187-*c*.1220	Restoration of Cathedral following the fire
1199	Cathedral re-dedicated
c.1225	Side chapels added to Cathedral south side
c.1250	Central tower heightened
1253-92	St Mary's Hospital built on current site
1262	Bishop Richard canonised
c.1275	Side chapels added to Cathedral north side
1276	St Richard's remains moved to shrine in retrochoir
1279-80	Greyfriars built as chancel of larger building
1288-1305	Lady Chapel added to Cathedral and eastern Norman bays of Cathedral rebuilt in Gothic style
1315	Tracery added to south transept window
1320	Choir stalls added
c.1400	Vicar's Hall and spire added
c.1410	Arundel screen built
1436	Cloisters and bell tower added
1501	Market Cross built
1538	St Richard's shrine destroyed
1636	North west tower collapsed
1642	Cathedral siezed by Parliammentary forces
1696	Ede's House built
c.1712	Pallant House built
1772-83	City gates removed
1807-8	Market House (Buttermarket) built
1812-13	St John the Evangelist built

1818-22	Chichester Canal built
1832-3	Corn Exchange built
1846	Railway arrives
1848-52	St Peter the Great built
1859	Arundel screen removed
1861	Cathedral spire collapsed in a gale
1866	Rebuilding of tower and spire complete
1930	Shrine to St Richard re-established
1947	Greyfriars becomes a museum
1962	Chichester Festival Theatre opens
1976	Chichester Centre of Arts opened
1982	Pallant House becomes part of Pallant House Gallery
1989	Minerva Theatre opens

Glossary

Apsidal	Semicircular or polygonal termination.
Canon	Clergyman belonging to Cathedral chapter or collegiate church.
Canonry	House or dwelling occupied by a canon.
Chantry Chapel	A chapel built to enable Masses to be said for the the soul of a deceased person.
Chapter	Assemblies of those responsible for the business, administration and discipline of the Cathedral.
Classical	Architectural style derived from the buildings of ancient Greece and Rome which was popular during the Renaissance and in Britain during the eighteenth century.
Cloister	A covered passageway between the Cathedral and its associated buildings that is usually square in plan, has a solid outer wall and is open with decorative tracery on the inner side.
Column	Vertical support used in Classical architecture.
Cornice	Uppermost part of an Entablature.
Dean	Head of the Cathedral chapter.
Decorated	The architectural style prevalent between *c*.1290 and *c*.1350.
Early English	The architectural style prevalent between *c*.1180 and *c*.1290 and epitomised by the use of plain, un-cusped lancet windows.
Entablature	The group of horizontal members, including the frieze and cornice, used in Classical architecture.
Frieze	Part of the entablature.
Gargoyle	A water spout which is decorated with carving depicting an animal or human head.
Georgian	General term used to describe the style of architecture which was popular during the reign of the four Georges (1714-1830) though often also used to cover the period from 1700 until Victoria came to the throne in 1837. The main styles covered in this period were Palladianism and neo-Classicism.
Gothic	The architectural style of the late twelfth to the mid-sixteenth century, characterised by pointed arches, clustered piers, window tracery, pinnacles, spires and soaring verticality. Medieval builders had no such term for their work; it was invented later. Yet later again British writers subdivided it into Early English, Decorated and Perpendicular.
Lay Vicar	Non-ordained member of the Cathedral choir.
neo-Classical	Style of Classical architecture popular in the second half of the eighteenth century which applied ancient precedents in a much freer manner than was possible under Palladianism.
Palladian	An architectural style that was derived from that used by Andrea Palladio (1508-80) which was popular in Britain between 1615 and

	1660s. Neo-Palladianism was a revival which was strongest during the first 50 years of the 1700s.
Prebendary	A clergyman who receives an stipend from a Cathedral or collegiate church.
Perpendicular	Architectural style developed from *c*.1330 and in use untill the middle of the sixteenth century. It is generally characterised by strong vertical tracery panels and a four-centered arch.